Arthur L. Atkins

Cyclist's Road Book of Boston and Vicinity

Second Edition

Arthur L. Atkins

Cyclist's Road Book of Boston and Vicinity
Second Edition

ISBN/EAN: 9783337417178

Printed in Europe, USA, Canada, Australia, Japan

Cover: Foto ©Andreas Hilbeck / pixelio.de

More available books at **www.hansebooks.com**

SECOND EDITION.

CYCLIST'S

ROAD · BOOK ⁕

❖ ❖ ❖ ❖ *OF ·BOSTON*

AND VICINITY.

BY.

A. L. ATKINS,

Consul for Boston, League of American
Wheelmen.

BOSTON:
PRINTED FOR THE AUTHOR.
1886.

INDEX.

SINGER'S CYCLES.

APOLLO BICYCLE.

Ball-Bearing Head, Double Balls to Front Wheel.

LIGHTEST AND MOST RIGID.

SINGER'S STRAIGHT STEERER

FASTEST TRICYCLE BUILT.

TANDEMS.

Springfield and Traveller.

EXAMINE BEFORE BUYING.

Catalogues Free.

W. B. EVERETT & Co..

6 & 8 BERKELEY ST., BOSTON, MASS.

That a road book, even an imperfect one, is a necessary adjunct to the paraphernalia of the intelligent wheelman, was fully substantiated by the cordial reception given the pioneer issue of the Cyclist's Road Book of Boston. Encouraged by the apparent appreciation of so many road riding wheelmen, the author again places at their disposal a second and enlarged edition of his work, in which he hopes that the mistakes and shortcomings of the first issue have been corrected, and that it possesses several improvements of practical value.

It is naturally probable that no book of this class could be compiled, even with the most searching care, which would be free of minor mistakes, and the author would consider it a marked favor if the discoverer of any mis-statement would report it to him, in order that it may be corrected in next season's edition.

In substance the arrangement of the first edition has been retained, the turnings specified as *right* or *left*, the distances stated, the condition of the road-bed given, and information calculated to be of interest to wheelmen is plentifully scattered throughout the book.

When two or more partially similar routes appear it is to be presumed that each presents an attraction or advantage unpossessed by the others.

The author again would express his appreciation of the very material aid rendered him by fellow wheelmen.   A. L. A.

No. 597 Washington street, Boston, Mass.,
May 20, 1886.

REPAIRING OF ALL KINDS.

1886

ROUTE ONE.

BOSTON TO CHESTNUT HILL RESERVOIR VIA HIGH-
LANDS.

	Trinity Sq.	
	Dartmouth St.	*Excellent.*
Right.	Columbus Ave.	*Asphalt.*
Left.	West Chester Park.	*Excellent.*
Right.	Harrison Ave.	*Good.*
Left.	Warren St. ⎫	"
Right.	Walnut Ave. ⎪	*Excellent.*
Right.	School St. ⎬ Highlands.	"
Left.	Amory St. ⎭	"
	BOYLSTON STATION.	3 1-2 miles.
	Boylston St.	*Excellent.*
Left.	Chestnut St.	"
Right.	Spring Park Ave.	"
	JAMAICA PLAIN.	4 miles.
Left.	Centre St.	*Excellent.*
Right.	Pond St.	"
Right.	Newton St.	"
Right.	Hammond St.	"
Right.	Beacon St.	"
	Rear Entrance.	9 3-4 miles.

The Reservoir drive is exceedingly popular among cyclists, who generally congregate at the watering-trough, at the lower basin. The Drive is also generally utilized as a training-track for Boston crack riders. It was at this place that G. R. Agassiz won the championship mile, in 3 21 1-2; and R. S. Codman made the quarter-mile record for the country, in 38 5-8 seconds, at the Suffolk Bicycle Club races, in the earlier days of cycling. The Drive of the lower-basin measures 1 1-6 (1.17) miles in the middle of the way, with the scratch at the watering-trough. The bicycle record of the Reservoir is held by E. P. Burnham, in 3.15; and the tricycle record by W. A. Rhodes, in 3.43.

ROUTE TWO.

BOSTON TO CHESTNUT HILL RESERVOIR VIA
BRIGHTON.

	Trinity Sq.	
	Dartmouth St.	*Excellent.*
Left.	Beacon St. ⎫ Mill-dam and	"
Right.	Brighton Ave. ⎬ Mile ground.	"
Left.	Cambridge St. ⎭	"

	BRIGHTON.	4¾ miles.
Left.	Winship St.	*Excellent.*
	Chestnut Hill Ave.	"
	Main Entrance.	5 miles.

[See notes to Route 1.]

This is the regular route out from the city. Although somewhat round-about it is far better than the more direct, viz: Beacon St. On Cambridge St., just beyond Winthrop St., is the Faneuil House, the League Hotel for Brighton.

ROUTE THREE.

CHESTNUT HILL RESERVOIR TO BOSTON VIA BROOKLINE AND LONGWOOD.

	Main Entrance.	
Right.	Chestnut Hill Ave.	*Excellent.*
Left.	Englewood Ave. (Coast.)	"
Left.	Beacon St. ⎱	*Good.*
Right.	Marion St. (Coast.) Brookline	*Excellent.*
Left.	Harvard St. ⎰	"
Right.	Sewall Ave. ⎱	"
Left.	Kent St.	"
Right.	Dudley St. Long-	"
Left.	Hawes St. wood.	"
Right.	Monmouth St.	"
Left.	St. Mary's St. ⎰	"
Right.	Brighton Ave. (Mill-dam.)	"
	Beacon St.	"
Right.	Dartmouth St.	"
	Trinity Sq.	5 miles.

This is one of the finest and most popular routes about Boston, its many turnings leading one through cool and shady avenues, lined by many of the finest suburban residences. It is a favorite return route for Reservoir moonlight parties.

ROUTE FOUR.

CHESTNUT HILL RESERVOIR TO COREY HILL.

	Main Entrance.	
Right.	Chestnut Hill Ave.	*Excellent.*
Left.	Englewood Ave. (Coast.)	"
Left.	Beacon St.	*Good.*
Left.	Summit Hill Ave. ⎱	
Left.	Corey Hill. ⎰	1 1-2 miles.

ROUTE FIVE.

BOSTON TO COREY HILL.

	Trinity Sq.	
	Dartmouth St.	*Excellent.*
Left.	Beacon St.	"
Right.	Summit Hill Ave. ⎱	"
	Corey Hill. ⎰	2 4-5 miles.

Return to Boston by Marion St., directly opposite, and Route 3.

Corey Hill was first overcome by Mr. H. D. Corey, of Boston, riding a Rudge; and subsequently by Mr. Bert Presey, of Smithville, N. J., riding a Star; Mr. E. R. Corson, of Rochester, N. H., riding a Star; Mr. Arthur Young, of St. Louis, Mo., riding an Expert Columbia; Mr. Joseph Murphy, of Waltham, Mass., riding a Standard Columbia; and Mr. W. W. Stall, of Boston, on a Victor tricycle. Prior to October, 1885, these gentlemen were the only cyclists who had succeeded in climbing the hill, but during that month a hill-climbing contest occurred, when seven bicyclists and four tricyclists reached the top. Mr. W. W. Stall, on a 54-inch Roadster Star, geared level, made the bicycle record for the hill in 3 m. 24 1-5 s.; and Mr. John Williams, on a 40-inch Quadrant tricycle, geared to 48 inches, secured the tricycle record, in 3 m. 46 2-5 s.

Length of Corey Hill, 2,300 feet; height 199 feet; average rise, 1 foot in 11.41; steepest grade, last 158 feet, 1 foot in 7.85.

The view from the top of the hill well repays for the labor of ascending it, on foot if necessary. The 158 feet is what generally bowls over the cyclists.

ROUTE S X.

BOSTON TO HARVARD SQUARE.

	Trinity Sq.		
	Dartmouth St.		*Excellent.*
Left.	Beacon St.	⎱ Mill-dam and	"
Right.	Brighton Ave.	⎰ Mile ground.	"
Right.	Linden St.		"
Right.	Cambridge St.		"
Left.	North Harvard St.		"
	Brighton St.		"
	Harvard Sq.		4 3-4 miles.

Return via Mt. Auburn St., *Right*, Magazine St., and the reverse of Route 8.

Harvard University joins Harvard Sq. Cyclists should especially inspect Hemenway Gymnasium, Memorial Hall, and the Washington Elm, on the north side of the Square.

ROUTE SEVEN.

BOSTON TO BEACON PARK.

	Trinity Sq.		
	Dartmouth St.		*Excellent.*
Left.	Commonwealth Ave.		*Good.*
Right.	Gloucester St.		"
Left.	Beacon St.	} Mill-dam and	*Excellent.*
Right.	Brighton Ave.	} Mile ground.	"
Right.	Harvard St.		"
Right.	Cambridge St.		"
	Allston Depot.		"
	Beacon Park.		3 3-4 miles.

The L. A. W. championship races, of '82, were held in the Park, as were also the once locally famous Boston and Massachusetts Inter-Club races. During the trotting season Beacon Park is the scene of many notable turf events.

ROUTE EIGHT.

BOSTON TO CAMBRIDGEPORT.

	Trinity Sq.		
	Dartmouth St.		*Excellent.*
Left.	Beacon St.	} Mill-dam and	"
Right.	Brighton Ave.	} Mile ground.	"
	Cottage Farm Bridge.		"
Right.	*Brookline Bridge.*		"
	Brookline St.		"
Left.	Chestnut St.		"
Right.	Magazine St.		*Good.*
	Central Sq.		3 1-4 miles.

Return, *Left*, River St. to ALLSTON STATION, Cambridge St., and reverse of Route 6.

The Harvard, Union and City rowing courses are in the Charles River on the right of Brookline bridge.

ROUTE NINE.

BOSTON TO BROOKLINE.

	Trinity Sq.	
	Dartmouth St.	*Excellent.*
Left.	Beacon St. ⎰ Mill-dam and	"
Right.	Brighton Ave. ⎱ Mile ground.	"
Left.	St. Mary's St.	"
Right.	Monmouth St. ⎰	"
Left.	Hawes St. ⎱	"
Right.	Colchester St. ⎰ Long-	"
Left.	Kent St. ⎱ wood.	"
Right.	Grove St. ⎰	"
Left.	Aspinwall St. ⎱	"
Left.	Harvard St.	"
	BROOKLINE.	3 3-8 miles.

Right.	Brighton Ave.	*Excellent.*
Left.	Harvard St.	"
	BROOKLINE.	4 1-4 miles.

Left.	Beacon St. (Mill-dam.)	*Excellent.*
Left.	Western Ave.	*Good.*
Right.	Tremont St.	"
	Walnut St.	"
	BROOKLINE.	3 1 8 miles.

RETURN.

	Walnut St.	*Good.*
Left.	Warren St.	"
Left.	Cottage St.	"
Left.	Goddard Ave.	"
Right.	Prince St.	"
Left.	Pond St.	"

And return to city by reverse of Route 1, or,

Right.	Warren St.	*Good.*
Left.	Boylston St.	"
Right.	Brighton St.	"
	Chestnut Hill Reservoir.	

And to Boston by Route 3, or reverse of Route 1 or 2.

The first section of this route leads through the handsomest part of the suburbs, and has somewhat of a gradual ascent all of the way. The second section is the best of the three, but is rather roundabout. The last section is the most direct, but is the poorest riding.

The Return Route includes several of the best of Boston roads, and is admirably adapted for an afternoon's spin.

ROUTE TEN.

BOSTON TO HOTEL FANEUIL.

	Trinity Sq.		
	Dartmouth St.		*Excellent.*
Left.	Beacon St.	} Mill-dam and	"
Right.	Brighton Ave.	} Mile ground.	"
Left.	Cambridge St.		"
	BRIGHTON.		
	Hotel Faneuil.		4 3-4 miles.

Hotel Faneuil, the League hotel for Brighton, is the recognized starting point of the long-distance road racing of Boston wheelmen. It was here that McCurdy, Munger, Huntley, Ives and Rhodes started and finished their contests in the fall of 1885. The hotel is well patronized by Sunday-riding cyclists and clubs on short moonlight runs.

ROUTE ELEVEN.

BOSTON TO MIDDLESEX FELLS AND SPOT POND.

	Trinity Sq.		
	Dartmouth St.		*Excellent.*
Left.	Beacon St.	} Mill-dam and	"
Right.	Brighton Ave.	} Mile ground.	"
Right.	Linden St.		"
Right.	Cambridge St.		"
Left.	North Harvard St.		"
	Brighton St.		"
Cross.	*Harvard Sq.*		4 3-4 miles.
	North Ave.		*Good.*
	PORTER'S STATION.		5 1-2 miles.
Right.	Russell St.		*Fair.*
Left.	Elm St.		"
Cross.	Broadway.		"
	Harvard St.		"
Left.	Medford St.		*Good.*
	MEDFORD.		8 3-4 miles.
Left.	*Forest St.*		*Good.*
	Middlesex Fells.	}	
	Spot Pond.	}	10 1-4 miles.

Return via WYOMING STATION and MALDEN, and reverse of Route 25.

A favorite resort for cycle picnics, and for participants in Sunday runs. There is no good hotel near by. Boats can be hired for rowing and sailing. The roads near the pond are quite hilly.   ·

ROUTE TWELVE.

BOSTON AROUND GREAT SIGN BOARDS.

	Trinity Sq.	
	Dartmouth St.	*Excellent.*
Left.	Commonwealth Ave.	"
Right.	West Chester Park.	*Good.*
Left.	Beacon St. ⎰ Mill-dam and	*Excellent.*
Right.	Brighton Ave. ⎱ Mile ground.	"
Left.	Cambridge St.	"
	BRIGHTON.	4 1-2 miles.
	Washington St.	*Good.*
	NEWTON.	6 3-4 miles.
	NEWTONVILLE.	7 3-4 miles.
	WEST NEWTON.	8 3-4 miles.
	Great Sign Boards.	10 1-2 miles.
Left.	Beacon St.	*Excellent.*
	Chestnut Hill Reservoir.	15 miles.

Return from the Reservoir by Route 3, or reverse of Route 1 or 2.

This route stands second in the favor of Boston wheelmen, and is especially utilized for moonlight and short club runs. The return into the Reservoir is a trifle hilly, but the road bed is of the very best, and the route includes many of the numerous superb country seats about Boston.

ROUTE THIRTEEN.

BOSTON TO SOMERVILLE.

	Trinity Sq.	
	Dartmouth St.	*Excellent.*
Left.	Beacon St. ⎰ Mill-dam and	"
Right.	Brighton Ave. ⎱ Mile ground.	"
	Cottage Farm Bridge.	
Right.	*Brookline Bridge.* `	

Left.	Chestnut St.	*Excellent.*
Right.	Magazine St.	"
Cross.	CAMBRIDGEPORT. } *Central Sq.* }	3 1 4 miles.
	Prospect St.	*Good.*
Left.	Webster Ave.	"
Cross.	*Railroad track.*	
	Union Sq. } SOMERVILLE. }	6 miles.

On Central Hill [via Summer St., *Right*, Walnut St., *Left*, Highland Ave.] is located the old fort, constructed partially of Revolutionary relics. The view from the hill embraces the adjoining towns for miles around.

ROUTE FOURTEEN.

BOSTON TO MT. AUBURN.

	Trinity Sq.	
	Dartmouth St.	*Excellent.*
Left.	Beacon St. } Mill-dam and	"
Right.	Brighton Ave. } Mile ground.	"
Right.	Linden St.	"
Right.	Cambridge St.	"
Left.	North Harvard St.	"
	Brighton St.	"
Left.	Mt. Auburn St.	*Good.*
	MT. AUBURN.	5 3-4 miles.

Mt. Auburn was established by the Massachusetts Horticultural Society in 1831, and is the oldest garden cemetery in America. Its horticultural beauties are upon the grandest scale.

ROUTE FIFTEEN.

BOSTON TO HUNNEWELL ESTATE.

	Trinity Sq.	
	Dartmouth St.	*Excellent.*
Left.	Beacon St. } Mill-dam and	"
Right.	Brighton Ave. } Mile ground.	"
Left.	Cambridge St.	"
Left.	Winship St.	"
Through Chestnut Hill Reservoir.		5 miles.

Right.	Beacon St.	*Excellent.*
	Great Sign Boards.	
	NEWTON LOWER FALLS.	10 miles.
	WELLESLEY HILLS.	11 1-2 miles.
	WELLESLEY.	13 1-4 miles.
Left.	Washington St.	*Good.*
	Hunnewell Estate.	14 1-2 miles.

The Hunnewell Estate is private, but the public is generally allowed access to the grounds, through the courtesy of Mr. Hunnewell, upon application at the mansion. The gardens are beautifully laid out after the English style, and overlook Lake Wauban and Wellesley College.

ROUTE SIXTEEN.

BOSTON TO RIDGE HILL FARM AND HOTEL WEL-
LESLEY.

[Baker's Gardens.]

	Trinity Sq.	
	Dartmouth St.	*Excellent.*
Left.	Beacon St. ⎱ Mill-dam and	"
Right.	Brighton Ave. ⎰ Mile ground.	"
Left.	Cambridge St.	
Left.	Winship St.	"
Through	*Chestnut Hill Reservoir.*	5 miles.
Right.	Beacon St.	*Excellent.*
	NEWTON CENTRE.	7 miles.
	Beacon St.	*Excellent.*
	NEWTON LOWER FALLS.	10 miles.
	WELLESLEY HILLS.	11 1-2 miles.
	WELLESLEY.	13 1-4 miles.
Left.	Grove St.	*Good.*
	Ridge Hill Farm. ⎱	
	Hotel Wellesley. ⎰	13 1-4 miles.

Ridge Hill Farm illustrates the peculiar style of its owner (W. E. Baker, Esq.), and is the field of strange conceits and remarkable out-of-door surprises.

ROUTE SEVENTEEN.

BOSTON TO ECHO BRIDGE, NEWTON.

	Trinity Sq.	
	Dartmouth St.	*Excellent.*
Left.	Beacon St. } Mill-dam and	"
Right.	Brighton Ave. } Mile ground.	"
Left.	Cambridge St.	"
Left.	Winship St.	"
Through Chestnut Hill Reservoir.		5 miles.
Right.	Beacon St.	*Excellent.*
	NEWTON CENTRE.	7 miles.
Left.	Centre St.	*Excellent.*
	NEWTON HIGHLANDS.	8 1-4 miles.
Right.	Boylston St.	*Excellent.*
Left.	*Echo Bridge.*	9 3-4 miles.

Try the echo under the bridge with the bugle. The
return route is abundant in magnificent coasts.

ROUTE EIGHTEEN.

BOSTON TO LEXINGTON VIA ARLINGTON.

	Trinity Sq.	
	Dartmouth St.	*Excellent.*
Left.	Beacon St. } Mill-dam and	"
Right.	Brighton Ave. } Mile ground.	"
Right.	Linden St.	"
Right.	Cambridge St.	"
Left.	North Harvard St.	"
	Brighton St.	"
Cross.	*Harvard Sq.*	4 3-4 miles.
	North Ave.	*Good.*
	PORTER'S STATION.	5 1-2 miles.
	ARLINGTON.	7 1-4 miles.
	Arlington Avenue.	*Poor.*
	EAST LEXINGTON.	10 1-4 miles.
	LEXINGTON (Common).	12 1-2 miles.
	Lexington Monument.	

Return via reverse of Route 20.

This route from North Ave. and beyond is substan-
tially the path taken by the British troops on the way
to the Battles of Lexington and Concord, and along the
road are many mementos of that Revolutionary event.
Route 20 gives much better wheeling, but is devoid of
historical points of interest.

ROUTE NINETEEN.

BOSTON TO HOTEL BOSCOBEL, LYNN.

[W. P. Comee, Proprietor.]

	Trinity Sq.	
	Dartmouth St.	*Excellent.*
Left.	Beacon St.	"
Right.	Brighton Ave.	"
Right.	Linden St.	"
Right.	Cambridge St.	"
Left.	North Harvard St.	"
	Brighton St.	"
	Harvard Sq.	"
	North Ave.	*Good.*
	PORTER'S STATION.	5 1-2 miles.
Right.	Russell St.	*Fair.*
Left.	Elm St.	"
Cross.	Broadway.	
	Harvard Sq.	*Good.*
Left.	Medford St.	"
	MEDFORD.	8 3-4 miles.
Right.	Salem St.	*Good.*
	MALDEN.	10 3-4 miles.
	MAPLEWOOD.	12 1-4 miles.
	EAST SAUGUS.	16 miles.
	LYNN.	
	Hotel Boscobel.	17 1-4 miles.

Beacon St. } Mill-dam and
Brighton Ave. } Mile ground.

The Boscobel is situated on the right at the head of
Lynn Common. It is specially arranged for the serv-
ing of club dinners, and a favorite resort for Sunday
tourists, who find in its dining room and on its cool
verandas the comforts of a model road house. This
house is extensively patronized by members of the
Cambridge, Somerville, Wakefield and other suburban
bicycle clubs. The Lynn bicycle track is reached from
the hotel by crossing through Elm Street and turning
to the right into Western Ave.

ROUTE TWENTY.

BOSTON TO LEXINGTON VIA WAVERLEY.

	Trinity Sq.	
	Dartmouth St.	*Excellent.*

Left.	Beacon St.	} Mill dam and	*Excellent.*
Right.	Brighton Ave.	} Mile ground.	"
Right.	Linden St.		"
Right.	Cambridge St.		"
Left.	North Harvard St.		"
	Brighton St.		"
Left.	Mt. Auburn St.		*Good.*
	MT. AUBURN.		5 3-4 miles.
	Belmont St.		*Fair.*
Right.	North St.		"
	WAVERLEY.		8 1-2 miles.
	EAST LEXINGTON.		11 1-2 miles.
Left.	*Main Road.*		*Fair.*
	LEXINGTON.		13 1-2 miles.

This route is about a mile longer than No. 18. The road bed is excellent, and it is recommended to those who prefer good riding to viewing historical landmarks.

ROUTE TWENTY-ONE.

BOSTON TO MASSAPOAG HOUSE, SHARON.

	Trinity Sq.	
	Dartmouth St.	*Good.*
Right.	Columbus Ave.	*Asphalt.*
Left.	W. Chester Park.	*Excellent.*
Right.	Harrison Ave.	*Good.*
Left.	Warren St.	"
Right.	Walnut Ave.	*Excellent.*
	Walnut St.	"
Right.	Morton St.	*Good.*
	Forest Hills Station.	3 1-2 miles.
Left.	Washington St.	*Good.*
	DEDHAM.	8 1-4 miles.
	East St.	*Good.*
Right.	Greenledge St.	*Fair.*
	Greenledge Station.	11 3-4 miles.
	Willow St.	*Fair.*
	Green St.	"
	Ponkapoag.	12 1-2 miles.
Right.	Washington St.	*Fair.*
	SOUTH CANTON.	16 1-4 miles.
	SHARON.	}
	Massapoag House.	} 20 miles.
	Lake Massapoag.	}

The "Wheel Around the Hub" tourists made the first night's stop at the Massapoag House. The roads beyond Dedham are somewhat below the average of suburban roads.

ROUTE TWENTY-TWO.

BOSTON TO CONCORD.

	Trinity Sq.	
	Dartmouth St.	*Excellent.*
Left.	Beacon St. } Mill-dam and	"
Right.	Brighton Ave. } Mile ground.	"
Right.	Linden St.	"
Right.	Cambridge St.	"
Left.	North Harvard St.	"
	Brighton St.	"
Cross.	*Harvard Sq.*	4 3-4 miles.
	PORTER'S STATION.	5 1-2 miles.
	ARLINGTON.	
	Arlington Ave.	*Poor.*
	EAST LEXINGTON.	6 1-2 miles.
	LEXINGTON (Common).	8 1-4 miles.
	Monument St.	*Poor.*
	Lexington St.	"
	CONCORD (Common).	14 1-2 miles.

About one mile this side of the Common is the old Nathaniel Hawthorne house (with tower), with Hawthorne's walk between it and the Alcott house, and the chapel of the Concord School of Philosophy adjoining. A half-mile further on, in the forks of the road, is the Emerson homestead. Just at the entrance to the village, on the left, is the old Wright Tavern. On the right, down Monument St., are the Old Manse and "One-Arch Bridge," the scene of the Battle of Concord. On Main St. are the Concord Library and the old Thoreau house, the present home of A. Bronson and Louisa M. Alcott. In the old Court House is the C. E. Davis collection of relics. The first Provincial Congress was held in the Unitarian Church edifice, near the Wright Tavern.

ROUTE TWENTY-THREE.

BOSTON TO CONCORD.

	Trinity Sq.		
	Dartmouth St.		*Excellent.*
Left.	Beacon St.	Mill-dam and	"
Right.	Brighton Ave.	Mile ground.	"
Right.	North Beacon St.		"
	Market St.		*Good.*
	WATERTOWN.		5 3-4 miles.
	Main St.		*Good.*
	WALTHAM.		8 3-4 miles.
	Main St.		*Good.*
Cross.	*Mass. Central R. R.*		
Right.	*Western Station.*		12 1-4 miles.
Left.	North Ave.		*Fair.*
Cross.	*Fitchburg R. R.*		
Right.	*Fork of Roads.*		"
Right.	Walden St.		*Poor.*
	Walden Pond.		
	CONCORD.		18 3-4 miles.

The excellence of the road-bed by this route over that of Route 22 more than compensates for the increased distance.

ROUTE TWENTY-FOUR.

BOSTON TO WAKEFIELD.

	Trinity Sq.		
	Dartmouth St.		*Excellent.*
Left.	Beacon St.	Mill-dam and	"
Right.	Brighton Ave.	Mile ground.	"
Right.	Linden St.		"
Right.	Cambridge St.		"
Left.	North Harvard St.		"
	Brighton St.		"
Cross.	*Harvard Sq.*		4 3-4 miles.
Left.	North Ave.		*Good.*
	PORTER'S STATION.		5 1-2 miles.
Right.	Russell St.		*Fair.*
Left.	Elm St.		"
Cross.	Broadway.		
	Harvard St.		"
Left.	Medford St.		*Good.*
	MEDFORD.		8 1-4 miles.

Right.	Salem St.	*Good.*
	MALDEN.	10 3-4 miles.
	Main St.	*Good.*
	MELROSE.	12 1-2 miles.
	Main St.	*Good.*
	WAKEFIELD.	16 1-4 miles.

This route passes Tufts College on the left. Mystic Trotting Park is on the right of Medford St. On Elm St., Somerville, is located the old Revolutionary powder house.

ROUTE TWENTY-FIVE.

BOSTON TO ESSEX HOUSE, SALEM.

	Trinity Sq.	
	Dartmouth St.	*Excellent.*
Left.	Beacon St. (Mill-dam and	"
Right.	Brighton Ave. } Mile ground.	"
Right.	Linden St.	"
Right.	Cambridge St.	"
Left.	North Harvard St.	"
	Brighton St.	"
Cross.	*Harvard Sq.*	4 3-4 miles.
Left.	North Ave.	*Good.*
	PORTER'S STATION.	5 1-2 miles.
Right.	Russell St.	*Fair.*
Left.	Elm St.	"
Cross.	Broadway.	"
	Harvard St.	"
Left.	Medford St.	*Good.*
	MEDFORD.	8 3-4 miles.
Right.	Salem St.	*Good.*
	MALDE .	10 3-4 miles.
	Salem St.	*Good.*
	MAPLEWOOD.	12 1-4 miles.
	EAST SAUGUS.	16 miles.
	LYNN (Common).	17 1-4 miles.
	Common St.	*Fair.*
	Essex St.	"
	Lafayette St.	*Good.*
Right.	Essex St.	"
	Essex House, SALEM.	

At Malden pump take Ferry St., *Left,* Elm St., for Woodlawn Cemetery.

This is one of the favorite runs for Boston wheelmen.

and one is always likely to find wheelmen, at dinner, at the Essex House. This route can be somewhat short-ened by taking the Chelsea Ferry, between Boston and Chelsea. [See last part of Route 42.]

An excellent after dinner trip can be made by crossing the bridge into Beverly, and on to Manchester and Gloucester, following the shore road. For points of interest in and about Gloucester read "In and Around Cape Ann," by J. S. Webber, Jr., of Gloucester.

ROUTE TWENTY-SIX.

BOSTON TO UNION MARKET HOUSE.

	Trinity Sq.	
	Dartmouth St.	*Excellent.*
Left.	Beacon St. } Mill-dam and	"
Right.	Brighton Ave. } Mile ground.	"
Right.	North Peacon St.	"
	Charles River Bridge.	
	United States Arsenal.	
Right.	Walnut St.	"
Left.	*Union Market House.*	5 1-4 miles.

This route is often chosen by the Mass. Bi. Club for a breakfast run. The Union House can be telephoned from Boston. The hotel is much patronized by cattle-dealers, and its substantial *cuisine*, particularly steaks and other meats, has earned a well-deserved reputation among the always hungry cyclists.

ROUTE TWENTY-SEVEN.

BOSTON TO WOODLAWN PARK HOTEL.

	Trinity Sq.	
	Dartmouth St.	*Excellent.*
Left.	Beacon St. } Mill-dam and	"
Right.	Brighton Ave. } Mile ground.	"
Left.	Cambridge St.	"
	BRIGHTON.	
	Washington St.	*Good.*
	NEWTON.	6 3-4 miles.
	NEWTONVILLE.	7 3-4 miles.
	WEST NEWTON.	8 3-4 miles.
	Washington St.	*Good.*
	Woodlawn Park Hotel.	9 1-2 miles.

Return via "Great Sign Boards" and Beacon St. to Chestnut Hill Reservoir, as given in Routes 3 and 12.

The Woodlawn Park Hotel is so much patronized by Massachusetts Bicycle Club men that it is frequently called the country headquarters of that Club. It is the rule for wheelmen to dine at the Woodlawn Park Hotel, when in the vicinity, and it is seldom that during the riding season one cannot find wheelmen there.

ROUTE TWENTY-EIGHT.

BOSTON TO BAILEY'S HOTEL, SOUTH NATICK.

	Trinity Sq.	
	Dartmouth St.	*Excellent.*
Left.	Beacon St. ⎰ Mill-dam and	"
Right.	Brighton Ave. ⎱ Mile ground.	"
Left.	Cambridge St.	"
Left.	Winship St.	"
Through Chestnut Hill Reservoir.		5 miles.
Right.	Beacon St.	*Excellent.*
	Great Sign Boards.	10 miles.
	NEWTON LOWER FALLS.	10 3-4 miles.
	WELLESLEY HILLS.	12 1-2 miles.
Left.	Washington St.	*Good.*
	SOUTH NATICK.	16 miles.
	Bailey's Hotel.	

Bailey's Hotel is the starting place of the 100 miles road and tricycle races of the Boston Bicycle Club, and the general rallying and dining place for all-day runs on Sundays and holidays. The vicinity of the hotel is rich in historical points of interest. In the square where now stands the drinking fountain once stood the oak under which John Eliot, the Indian apostle, week'y gathered together the first Indian Church, after the flight from Nonantum Hill. A large tree near by goes by the name of "Eliot's Oak," in commemoration of these meetings, and directly opposite the hotel, in the green, stands the Eliot Memorial Monument. The roads into the city are of the very highest sand-papered variety, and are the chosen scorching grounds of the city "cracks."

ROUTE TWENTY-NINE.

BOSTON TO COBB'S TAVERN.

Trinity Sq.	
Dartmouth St.	*Good.*

Right.	Columbus Ave.	*Asphalt.*
Left.	W. Chester Park.	*Excellent.*
	Swett St.	*Good.*
Right.	Boston St.	"
	Columbia St.	"
Left.	Washington St.	"
	Codman Hill.	(*Coast carefully.*)
	DORCHESTER.	6 1-4 miles.
Cross	*Neponset River Bridge.*	
	MILTON LOWER MILLS.	6 1-2 miles.
	Milton Hill.	
Right.	Centre Ave.	*Good.*
	Washington St.	"
Right.	Washington St.	"
	Cemetery.	
	Cobb's Tavern.	14 miles.

At the top of Milton Hill an excellent view of Boston
Harbor and Massachusetts Bay, and of the surrounding
country, is afforded. Codman Hill has a short stiff
grade which should be coasted carefully. Cobb's
Tavern is sometimes styled the country house of the
Boston Bicycle Club, it being the turning point of the
majority of its club runs. The hotel building has the
appearance of a farm house of a century ago.

ROUTE THIRTY.

BOSTON TO SOUTH ABINGTON AND BROCKTON.

	Trinity Sq.	
	Dartmouth St.	*Good.*
Right.	Columbus Ave.	*Asphalt.*
Left.	Chester Park.	*Excellent.*
Right.	Boston St.	*Good.*
Left.	Hancock St.	"
Left.	Adams St.	*Excellent.*
Left.	Neponset Ave.	*Fair.*
	WOLLASTON HEIGHTS.	9 1-4 miles.
	QUINCY.	10 3-4 miles.
	WEYMOUTH LANDING.	13 1-4 miles.
	SO. WEYMOUTH.	16 1-4 miles.
	NO. ABINGTON.	19 1-4 miles.
	ABINGTON.	21 miles.
	SO. ABINGTON.	23 miles.
	BROCKTON.	28 miles.

ROUTE THIRTY-ONE.

BOSTON TO WEST ROXBURY PARK.

	Trinity Sq.	
	Dartmouth St.	*Good.*
Right.	Columbus Ave.	*Asphalt.*
Left.	Chester Park.	*Excellent.*
Right.	Harrison Ave.	*Good.*
Left.	Warren St.	"
Right.	Blue Hill Ave.	"
	WEST ROXBURY PARK.	3 3-4 miles.

Return, *Right,* Morton or Williams St. to Walnut Ave., and to city by reverse of Route 1.

The land occupied by West Roxbury Park, which has recently been purchased by the City, covers about 500 acres of more or less wild fields and wood-lands. The City has begun improvements, but it will be several years, probably, before any material change will be made over the natural appearance of this territory, and cyclists have full access to the roads which existed before the land became public property. On holidays the Park is the scene of much enlivenment, with numerous picnics and band concerts.

ROUTE THIRTY-TWO.

BOSTON TO MILTON AND QUINCY.

	Trinity Sq.	
	Dartmouth St.	*Good.*
Right	Columbus Ave.	*Asphalt.*
Left.	W. Chester Park.	*Excellent.*
Left.	Swett St.	*Good.*
Right.	Boston St.	"
	Columbia St.	"
Left	Washington St.	*Excellent.*
	Codman Hill.	(*Coast carefully.*)
	DORCHESTER.	6 1-4 miles.
	Neponset River Bridge.	
	MILTON LOWER MILLS.	6 1-2 miles.
	Milton Hill.	
	Adams St.	*Excellent.*
	EAST MILTON.	8 1-4 miles.
	Blue Bell.	
	QUINCY.	11 1-2 miles.

Codman Hill is a short sharp coast, use care. Milton Hill is a very hard climb, and should only be coasted by skilful riders, and with brake on. Quincy is the home of the Adams family, and in the neighborhood are many points of historical interest, especially connected with the "Family of Presidents."

ROUTE THIRTY-THREE.

BOSTON TO MATTAPAN.

	Trinity Sq.	
	Dartmouth St.	Good.
Right.	Columbus Ave.	Asphalt.
Left.	W. Chester Park.	Excellent.
Right.	Harrison Ave.	Good.
Left.	Warren St.	"
Right.	Walnut Ave.	Excellent.
Left.	Dale St.	"
Right.	Laurel St.	"
Left.	Tower St.	"
Right.	Warren St.	Good.
Left.	Washington St.	Excellent.
	DORCHESTER.	6 1-2 miles.
Right.	River St.	Excellent.
	MATTAPAN.	8 1-2 miles.

To return to Boston, continue on to Hyde Park, and then the reverse of Route 34.

The participants in "The Wheel Around the Hub," in 1880 and 1884, started from the corner of Warren St. and Walnut Ave. The roads in and around Mattapan are unusually excellent, and generally form a part of the road race courses.

ROUTE THIRTY-FOUR.

BOSTON TO ARNOLD ARBORETUM AND HYDE PARK.

	Trinity Sq.	
	Dartmouth St.	Good.
Right.	Columbus Ave.	Asphalt.
Left.	W. Chester Park.	Excellent.
Right.	Harrison Ave.	Good.
Left.	Warren St.	Good.
Right.	Walnut Ave.	Excellent.
Right.	Morton St.	Good.

	Forest Hills Station.	3 1-2 miles.
Cross.	Boston and Providence R. R.	
	Arnold Arboretum.	
	Bussey Farm.	5 1-2 miles.
Left.	Hyde Park Ave.	*Fair.*
	HYDE PARK.	6 1-2 miles.

Return from Arnold Arboretum, Walter St. to Pond St., Jamaica Plain, and reverse of Route 1; from Hyde Park, one good way is by River St. to Mattapan, and reverse of Route 33.

At the Arboretum and Farm is a nearly exhaustive collection of shrubs and herbaceous plants possible to be grown in the open air in this climate. The Bussey Farm is the agricultural and horticultural department of Harvard University.

ROUTE THIRTY-FIVE.

MILTON LOWER MILLS TO WEST AND SOUTH QUINCY.　•

	MILTON LOWER MILLS.	
	Adams St.	
	Milton Hill.	
	EAST MILTON STATION.	1 1-2 miles.
	RAILWAY VILLAGE.	2 miles.
Right.	Common St.	*Good.*
	WEST QUINCY.	3 1-2 miles.
Left.	Water St.	*Fair.*
Right.	Franklin St.	"
	SOUTH QUINCY.	5 miles.

At the foot of Franklin St. hill are located two old-fashioned houses, the birthplaces of John Adams and John Quincy Adams. From the top of Penn's Hill, close by, Mrs. John Adams and young Quincy Adams watched the Battle of Bunker Hill, and saw the departure of the British fleet from Boston. Scattered through the township of Quincy are many other historical points of interest pertaining to Revolutionary times, directly connected with the Adams and Hancock families.

ROUTE THIRTY-SIX.

BOSTON TO FOXBORO.

	Trinity Sq.	
	Dartmouth St.	*Good.*
Right.	Columbus Ave.	*Asphalt.*

Left.	Chester Park.	*Excellent.*
Right.	Harrison Ave.	*Good.*
Left.	Warren St.	"
Right.	Walnut Ave.	*Excellent.*
	Walnut St.	*Good.*
Right.	Morton St.	"
	FOREST HILLS STATION.	3 1-2 miles.
Cross.	*Railroad.*	
	Arnold Arboretum.	
	Bussey Farm.	
Right.	Bussey St.	*Good.*
Left.	Walter St.	"
	South St.	"
	WEST ROXBURY.	8 1-4 miles.
	DEDHAM.	10 3-4 miles.
	NORWOOD.	14 1-2 miles.
	EAST WALPOLE.	16 1-4 miles.
	WALPOLE.	19 miles.
	SOUTH WALPOLE.	22 1-4 miles.
	FOXBORO.	25 1-4 miles.

ROUTE THIRTY-SEVEN.

BOSTON TO BROCKTON.

	Trinity Sq.	
	Dartmouth St.	*Good.*
Right.	Columbus Ave.	*Asphalt.*
Left.	Chester Park.	*Excellent.*
Right.	Harrison Ave.	*Good.*
Left.	Hunneman St.	*Fair.*
	Yeoman St.	"
	Norfolk Ave.	"
	Cottage Ave.	"
Right.	Boston St.	*Good.*
Left.	Hancock St.	"
Left.	Adams St.	*Excellent.*
	DORCHESTER.	8 1-4 miles.
Cross.	*Neponset River Bridge.*	
	MILTON LOWER MILLS.	8 1-2 miles.
	Milton Hill.	
	Adams St.	*Excellent.*
	EAST MILTON.	11 1-4 miles.
	QUINCY.	13 3-4 miles.
	BRAINTREE.	15 1-4 miles.
	SOUTH BRAINTREE.	17 miles.
	RANDOLPH.	20 1-4 miles.
	BROCKTON.	25 2-5 miles.

ROUTE THIRTY-EIGHT.

BOSTON TO NANTASKET BEACH.

	Trinity Sq.	
	Dartmouth St.	*Good.*
Right.	Columbus Ave.	*Asphalt.*
Left.	Chester Park.	*Excellent.*
Right.	Harrison Ave.	*Good.*
Left.	Warren St.	"
Left.	Washington St.	"
	Codman Hill.	(*Coast carefully.*)
	DORCHESTER.	6 1-4 miles.
Cross.	*Neponset River Bridge.*	
	MILTON LOWER MILLS.	6 1-2 miles.
	Milton Hill.	
	Adams St.	*Excellent.*
	EAST MILTON.	8 miles.
	QUINCY.	10 1-2 miles.
	Washington St.	*Good.*
	QUINCY POINT.	12 1-4 miles.
	NORTH WEYMOUTH.	14 miles.
	Bridge St.	*Fair.*
	Lincoln St.	"
	HINGHAM.	17 miles.
	Old Colony House.	
	Rockland St.	*Fair.*
	NANTASKET P. O.	19 1-4 miles.

At Nantasket P. O., take Jerusalem Road to the right, for shore hotels and restaurants in Cohasset; and to the left for Nantasket Beach resorts. The roads in the vicinity of the beach are more or less sandy, particularly so in dry weather.

The return to Boston can be made by cars or steamer.

ROUTE THIRTY-NINE.

BOSTON TO DOWNER'S LANDING.

	Trinity Sq.	
	Dartmouth St.	*Good.*
Right.	Columbus Ave.	*Asphalt.*
Left.	Chester Park.	*Excellent.*
Right.	Harrison Ave.	*Good.*
Left.	Warren St.	"
Left.	Washington St.	*Excellent.*
	Codman Hill.	(*Coast carefully.*)

	DORCHESTER.	6 1-4 miles.
Cross.	*Neponset River Bridge.*	
	MILTON LOWER MILLS.	6 1-2 miles.
	Milton Hill.	
	Adams St.	*Excellent.*
	EAST MILTON.	8 miles.
	QUINCY.	10 1-2 miles.
	Washington St.	*Good.*
	QUINCY POINT.	12 1-4 miles.
	NORTH WEYMOUTH.	14 miles.
	Bridge St.	*Good.*
	Lincoln St.	"
	HINGHAM.	17 miles.
	Bridge St.	*Good.*
	Squirrel Hill.	
	DOWNER'S LANDING, first street on the left.	
		18 3-4 miles.

Downer's Landing is a seashore summer resort in Boston Harbor, and its clam and fish dinners are popular with cyclists, particularly members of the Boston Bicycle Club. In dry weather especially the roads in this vicinity are very sandy.

ROUTE FORTY.

BOSTON TO BUNKER HILL MONUMENT.

	Trinity Sq.	
	Dartmouth St.	*Excellent.*
Left.	Beacon St. } Mill-dam and	"
Right.	Brighton Ave. } Mile ground.	"
Right.	Linden St.	"
Right.	Cambridge St.	"
Left.	North Harvard St.	"
	Brighton St.	"
Cross.	*Harvard Sq.*	4 3-4 mile
Right.	Kirkland St.	*Good.*
	Washington St.	"
	Union Sq. }	
	SOMERVILLE. }	5 miles.
	Washington St.	*Good.*
	Sullivan Sq. }	
	CHARLESTOWN. }	6 1-4 miles
Right.	Rutherford St.	*Good*
Left.	Austin St.	"
Cross.	Main St.	*Poor.*

Right.	Warren St.	*Good.*
Left.	Monument Ave.	"
	MONUMENT.	7 1-2 miles.

The monument is located in the centre of Charlestown, and is reached by this route without passing over any paved or poor streets.

ROUTE FORTY-ONE.

BOSTON TO REVERE BEACH, POINT OF PINES, BEACH-
MONT, OCEAN SPRAY, GREAT HEAD
AND POINT SHIRLEY.

	Trinity Sq.	
	Dartmouth St.	*Excellent.*
Left.	Beacon St. } Mill-dam and	"
Right.	Brighton Ave. } Mile ground.	"
Right.	Linden St.	"
Right.	Cambridge St.	"
Left.	North Harvard St.	"
	Brighton St.	"
Cross.	*Harvard Sq.*	4 3-4 miles.
Left.	North Ave.	*Good.*
	PORTER'S STATION.	5 1-2 miles.
Right.	Russell St.	*Fair.*
Left.	Elm St.	"
Cross.	Broadway.	"
	Harvard St.	"
Left.	Medford St.	*Good.*
	MEDFORD.	8 3-4 miles.
Right.	Salem St.	*Good.*
	MALDEN.	10 3-4 miles.
	MAPLEWOOD.	12 1-4 miles.
	Linden Sq.	*Good.*
Right.	Washington Ave.	"
Left.	Malden St.	"
Left.	Beach St.	"
	Depot.	5 miles.
Right.	Beach Road.	
	{ OCEAN PIER.	
	{ BEACHMONT.	
To	{ OCEAN SPRAY.	
	{ GREAT HEAD.	
	{ POINT SHIRLEY.	
	{ SUNNY SIDE.	
Left.	Beach road (*very poor*) at Depot, for	

> *Revere Beach.*
> *Point of Pines.*
>
> *East Boston North Ferry.*
> EAST BOSTON.
> Maverick Sq.
> Meridian St.   *Good.*

Right.	Saratoga St.	"
Right.	WINTHROP JUNCTION.	
	Bridge.	
	WINTHROP.	
	OCEAN SPRAY.	

To return from Ocean Spray, cross the bridge at Great Head, run through Winthrop village, to the bridge, and to Winthrop Junction.

All of these places lie along the North Shore, and are about a mile apart. The Point of Pines is a famous sea-side resort, with skating rink and band concerts afternoon and evening, and illuminations at night, and other sea-side attractions in abundance.

Boston can be reached from all of these resorts by frequent trains.

ROUTE FORTY-TWO.

BOSTON TO NAHANT.

	Trinity Sq.	
	Dartmouth St.	*Excellent.*
Left.	Beacon St. } Mill-dam and	"
Right.	Brighton Ave. } M le ground.	"
Right.	Linden St.	"
Right.	Cambridge St.	"
Left.	North Harvard St.	"
	Brighton St.	"
Cross.	Harvard Sq.	4 3-4 miles.
Left.	North Ave.	*Good.*
	PORTER'S STATION.	5 1-2 miles.
Right.	Russell St.	*Fair.*
Left.	Elm St.	"
Cross.	Broadway.	
	Harvard St.	"
Left.	Medford St.	*Good.*
	MEDFORD.	8 3-4 miles.
Right.	Salem St.	*Good.*
	MALDEN.	10 3-4 miles.
	MAPLEWOOD.	12 1-4 "
	EAST SAUGUS.	16 "

	LYNN (Common).	17 1-4 miles.
	North or South Common St.	*Good.*
Right.	Market St.	"
Left.	Broad St.	"
Right.	Newhall St.	"
Right.	Lower Beach Road.	"
	Hood Cottage. *Bass Point House.* } NAHANT.	20 1-4 miles.
	Relay House.	

At Malden Pump take Ferry St., *Left*, Elm St., for Woodlawn Cemetery.

This Route can be considerably shortened by taking Chelsea Ferry (foot of Hanover St.) to Chelsea, and as follows:

	Chelsea Ferry.	
	CHELSEA.	
	Winnisimmit St.	*Poor.*
Left.	Beacon St.	*Fair.*
Right.	Chestnut St. (*Coast.*)	*Good.*
Left.	Fifth St.	"
Right.	Spruce St.	"
Right.	Washington Ave.	*Fair.*
	Carey Ave.	*Good.*
Left.	Clarke Ave.	"
Right.	Eleanor St.	"
Left.	Broadway.	"
	REVERE.	
	LYNN (Common.)	

Nahant is a beautiful and aristocratic watering place, with superb ocean views and breezes. The ocean roads are very good. The points of interest are Pirates' Cave, Maolis Gardens, Natural Bridge, Pulpit Rock, Spouting Horn and Cauldron Cliff.

ROUTE FORTY-THREE.

BAILEY'S HOTEL TO ECHO BRIDGE, VIA SOUTH BANK OF CHARLES RIVER.

	Bailey's Hotel. SOUTH NATICK. }	
Cross.	*Charles River at* Pleasant St.	*Good.*
Pass.	*Charles River St.*	"
Left.	South Bank River Road.	"
Cross.	*Charles River.*	

	Central Ave.	Fair.
	NEEDHAM.	4 3-4 miles.
	NEWTON UPPER FALLS.	7 1-4 miles.
	Echo Bridge.	

ROUTE FORTY-FOUR.

BAILEY'S HOTEL, SOUTH NATICK, TO NEWTON CENTRE, VIA NORTH BANK OF CHARLES RIVER.

	Bailey's Hotel. }	
	SOUTH NATICK. }	
	Pleasant St.	Good.
Cross.	Charles River.	
Left.	Charles River St.	"
	Pine St.	Fair.
	Central Ave.	"
Right.	Great Plain Ave.	"
	NEEDHAM PLAINS.	5 miles.
Left.	Highland Ave.	Fair.
	HIGHLANDVILLE.	5 3-4 miles.
	NEWTON HIGHLANDS.	8 miles.
	Centre St.	Fair.
	NEWTON CENTRE.	9 miles.

ROUTE FORTY-FIVE.

SOUTH NATICK TO FRAMINGHAM AND SOUTHBORO.

	Bailey's Hotel. }	
	SOUTH NATICK. }	
	Union St.	Excellent.
	NATICK.	2 miles.
	Lake Cochituate.	
	SOUTH FRAMINGHAM.	4 miles.
	Railroad Station.	
Cross.	Railroad Track.	
	Main Road.	Excellent.
	FRAMINGHAM CENTRE.	3 miles.
	Reservoir.	
Under	Railroad Bridge.	
	SOUTHBORO.	3 miles.

At Framingham Reservoir the "sand paper" district practically ends, yet the riding to Southboro and beyond is fair. The Deerfoot Farms are located at Southboro.

ROUTE FORTY-SIX.

TRINITY SQ. TO AUBURNDALE, VIA RESERVOIR ROAD.

	Trinity Sq.	
	Dartmouth St.	
Left.	Commonwealth Ave.	*Excellent.*
Right.	Gloucester St.	"
Left.	Beacon St. } Mill-dam and	"
Right.	Brighton Ave. } Mile ground.	"
Left.	Cambridge St.	*Good.*
Left.	Winship St.	"
Right.	South St.	"
Right.	Ward St.	"
Left.	Centre St.	"
Right.	Homer St.	"
	Fuller St.	*Fair.*
Left.	Washington St.	*Good.*
Right.	Woodlawn St.	"
	AUBURNDALE.	10 miles.

Return to Washington St., and via Newton to Boston.

ROUTE FORTY-SEVEN.

CHESTNUT HILL RESERVOIR TO NORFOLK HOUSE.

	DEDHAM.	
	Reservoir.	
	Beacon St.	*Good.*
Left.	Hammond St.	*Excellent.*
Left.	Newton St.	"
Right.	South St.	"
	Church St.	*Good.*
	South St.	"
Right.	Centre St.	"
	WEST ROXBURY.	5 1-4 miles.
Right.	Spring St.	*Good.*
	Charles River.	
	Bridge St.	
Left.	Ames Street.	*Good.*
	Charles River.	
	Washington St.	*Good.*
	Norfolk House. }	
	DEDHAM. }	7 3-4 miles.

The Norfolk House is well patronized by members of the Boston Club, and by parties from the Reservoir.

ROUTE FORTY-EIGHT.

MATTAPAN TO MASSAPOAG HOUSE, SHARON.

	MATTAPAN.	
	Blue Hill Ave.	*Good.*
Between.	{ Blue Hill.	
	{ Little Blue Hill.	
Right.	Washington St.	*Fair.*
Pass.	Dedham St.	"
Left.	Main Road.	"
Through	SOUTH CANTON.	8 1-2 miles.
Right.	Main St.	*Fair.*
	SHARON.	11 1-4 miles.
Left.	Pond St.	*Fair.*
	Massapoag House.	13 1-4 miles.

Pond St. and its extension circle the lake. The Massapoag House is a favorite stopping place for cyclists.

The view from the top of the highest of the Blue Hills surpasses any view in America of cultivated country scenery, combined with an extensive view of Boston and twenty or more towns, and the ocean. The horizon line encloses over 400 square miles of land and water.

ROUTE FORTY-NINE.

JAMAICA PLAIN TO WEST ROXBURY AND DEDHAM.

	Soldiers' Monument. }	
	JAMAICA PLAIN. }	
	Eliot St.	*Excellent.*
	Pond St.	"
	Pond St. Hill.	
	Newton St.	"
Left.	Grove St.	"
Left.	South St.	"
	Church St.	*Good.*
Right.	Centre St.	"
	WEST ROXBURY.	4 1-2 miles.
	DEDHAM.	7 miles.
For Boston take		
Left.	High St.	*Good.*
	MILL VILLAGE.	1 1-4 miles.
Right.	Milton St.	
Cross.	*Railroad Track.*	
Left.	Central Park Ave.	*Fair.*
	Hyde Park Ave.	"
	HYDE PARK.	3 1-2 miles.

	Forest Hills.	6 3-4 miles.
	For a better quality of road take at	
	Mill Village.	
	Milton St.	*Fair.*
Left.	River St.	*Good.*
	Hyde Park.	2 miles.
	Mattapan.	
	Milton Lower Mills.	4 3-4 miles.

[See Milton Lower Mills for Boston return routes.]

ROUTE FIFTY.

Chestnut Hill Reservoir to Mattapan, via Roslindale.

	Reservoir.	
	Beacon St.	*Good.*
Left.	Hammond St.	*Excellent.*
Left.	Newton St.	"
Right.	South St.	"
	Church St.	*Good.*
	South St.	"

At junction of Water and South Sts., turn sharply to the *Right*, by Roslindale Station, *Cross* Washington St. and Hyde Park Ave., then wheel directly to Mattapan, 7 1-4 miles. (See Mattapan in Index for several continuations of this route.

ROUTE FIFTY-ONE.

Chestnut Hill Reservoir to Arnold Arboretum.

	Reservoir.	
	Beacon St.	*Excellent.*
	Newton Centre.	2 miles.
Left.	Centre St.	
Left.	Parker St.	*Good.*
Left.	Dedham St.	"
Left.	Weld St.	"
	Arnold Arboretum.	7 1-2 miles.

ROUTE FIFTY-TWO.

Harvard Sq. to Woburn, via Middlesex Fells and Spot Pond.

	Harvard Sq.	
Left.	North Ave.	*Good.*
	Porter's Station.	

Right.	Russell St.	*Fair.*
Left.	Elm St.	"
Cross.	Broadway.	"
	Harvard St.	"
Left.	Medford St.	*Good.*
	MEDFORD.	5 miles.
Cross.	*Mystic River.*	
Left.	Fulton St.	*Good.*
	Wyoming St.	*Fair.*
	Pond St.	"
	Spot Pond.	8 miles.
Left.	Marble St.	*Fair.*
	EAST WOBURN.	10 3-4 miles.
Left.	Railroad St.	*Fair.*
	WOBURN.	12 1-4 miles.
Return,		
	Main St.	*Fair.*
	WINCHESTER.	2 miles.
	Wedge Pond.	
	Grove St.	*Fair.*
	WEST MEDFORD.	4 1-4 miles.

The region about Spot Pond is included under the comprehensive title of Middlesex Fells.

ROUTE FIFTY-THREE.

BOSTON TO READING.

	Trinity Sq.	
	Dartmouth St.	*Excellent.*
Left.	Beacon St. } Mill-dam and	"
Right.	Brighton Ave. } Mile ground.	"
Right.	Linden St.	"
Right.	Cambridge St.	"
Left.	North Harvard Street.	"
	Brighton St.	"
Cross.	Harvard Sq.	4 3-4 miles.
Left.	North Ave.	*Good.*
	PORTER'S STATION.	
Right.	Russell St.	*Fair.*
Left.	Elm St.	"
Cross.	Broadway.	"
	Harvard St.	"
Left.	Medford St.	"
	MEDFORD.	8 3-4 miles.
Cross.	*Mystic River.*	

Left.	Fulton St.	*Good.*
	Wyoming St.	*Fair.*
	Pond St.	"
Left.	South St.	"
	Main St.	"
	STONEHAM.	10 1-4 miles.
	Main St.	*Fair.*
	READING.	12 1-2 miles.
Return,		
	John St.	*Fair.*
	Lake Managowitt.	
	Green St.	"
	WAKEFIELD.	3 miles.
	Main St.	*Fair.*
	Crystal Lake.	
	GREENWOOD.	3 3-4 miles.
	MELROSE.	5 miles.
	MALDEN.	7 3-4 miles.

[See Malden for return to Boston.]

This route can be shortened by taking Forest Street to Reading direct, but the road-bed this way is very poor.

ROUTE FIFTY-FOUR.

BOSTON TO GLOUCESTER.

	Trinity Sq.	
	Dartmouth St.	*Excellent.*
Left.	Beacon St. } Mill-dam and	"
Right.	Brighton Ave. } Mile ground.	"
Right.	Linden St.	"
Right.	Cambridge St.	"
Left.	North Harvard St.	"
	Brighton St.	"
Cross.	*Harvard Sq.*	4 3-4 miles.
Left.	North Ave.	*Good.*
	PORTER'S STATION.	5 1-2 miles.
Right.	Russell St.	*Fair.*
Left.	Elm St.	"
Cross.	Broadway.	"
	Harvard St.	
Left.	Medford St.	*Good.*
	MEDFORD.	8 3-4 miles.
Right.	Salem St.	*Good.*
	MALDEN.	10 3-4 miles.

	Salem St.	Good.
	MAPLEWOOD.	12 1-4 miles.
	EAST SAUGUS.	16 miles.
	Lynn (Common).	7 1-4 miles.
	Common St.	Fair.
	Essex St.	"
	Lafayette St.	Good.
Right.	Essex St.	"
	Essex House, Salem.	22 1-2 miles.
Left.	St. Peter's St.	Good.
Right.	Brown St.	"
Left.	Winter St.	"
Right.	Bridge St.	"
	Bridge.	"
	Rantoul St.	"
	BEVERLY.	24 1-4 miles.
Right.	Pow St.	Good.
	Soldiers' Monument.	
Left.	Hale St.	"
	Pride's Crossing.	26 1-2 miles.
	BEVERLY FARMS.	27 miles.
	MANCHESTER.	29 3-4 miles.
	MAGNOLIA.	32 1-2 miles.
	GLOUCESTER.	37 miles.

The cycling headquarters hereabouts is located at the bicycle store of John Wood, Jr., Rantoul St. Mr. Wood is especially familiar with the roads and attractions in this vicinity, and is always happy to impart any information or to show courtesy to visiting cyclists.

ROUTE FIFTY-FIVE.

BEVERLY TO NEWBURYPORT.

	Depot Square.	
	Rantoul St.	Good.
Follow.	Horse-car Track.	
	No. Beverly.	
	Wenham.	
	Hamilton.	
	IPSWICH.	11 1-2 miles.
Right.	Engine House.	
Left.	First St.	Good.

	ROWLEY.	16 miles.
Cross.	*Bridge.*	
	NEWBURY.	
	Cemetery.	
	High St.	*Good.*
	Merrimac House. }	
	NEWBURYPORT. }	

This route was a part of the original 100 miles road race. The roads beyond Beverly are fully up to the average of country roads.

HARVARD PRESS,
Harvard Square, Cambridge
William B. Howland.

I. H. FARRINGTON,

Merchant Tailor,

386 WASHINGTON

AND

13 FRANKLIN STREET,

◁BOSTON.▷

Club Tailor Massachusetts Bicycle Club.

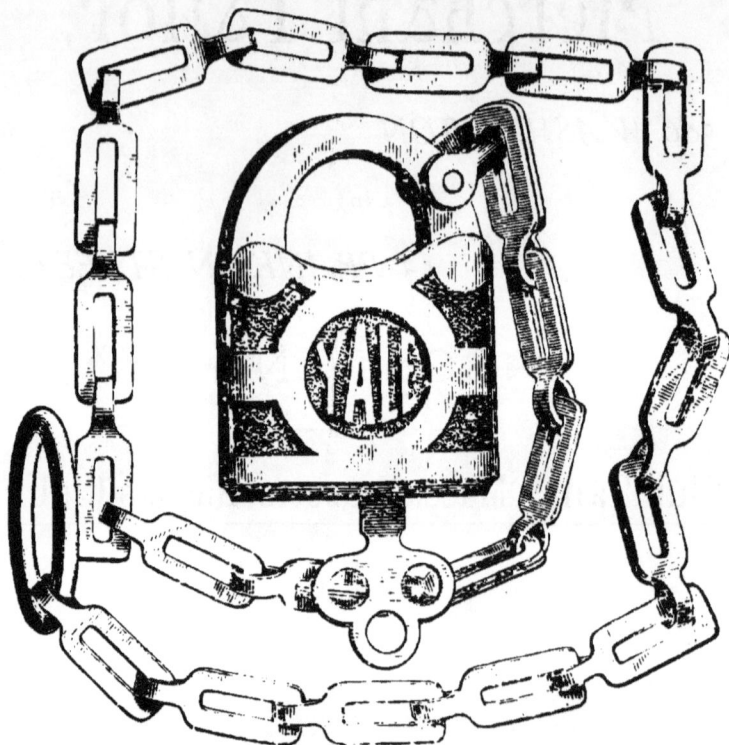

THE BUTCHER

CYCLOMETERS

OLDEST,

Most Reliable and Easiest to Read.

NO RIDER SHOULD BE WITHOUT

ONE OF T

VALUABLE INSTRUMENTS.

BUTCHER CYCLOMETER CO.,

6 and 8 Berkeley Street, Boston.

Call and have one put on your Wheel.

Hastings

THE PHOTOGRAPHER,
147 TREMONT ST. cor. WEST ST.

Is Not Excelled in the Quality of His Artistic Productions.

Everything in the line of

Photographic Work

FINISHED IN A SUPERIOR MANNER.

Elevator to Studio.

INSTANTANEOUS PROCESS USED.

CABINET PHOTOS ONLY $5.00 PER DOZ.

EASY STAIRS

For getting the Bicycle to the Studio.

SPECIAL INDUCEMENTS TO CLUBS.

Telephone 462.

Member of the Mass. and Newton Clubs.

Club Tailor to the Massachusetts and
Boston Clubs for

BICYCLE SUITS ✦ ✦
- - *IN EVERY STYLE*

MADE FROM THE BEST

ENGLISH SERGES & CASSIMERES

A FULL ASSORTMENT OF

FOREIGN AND DOMESTIC

WOOLLENS

Always on hand for gentlemen's fine wear, at moderate prices.

PACIFIC HOUSE,

NANTASKET BEACH, MASS.

—

HOWARD HOUSE,

RANDOLPH, MASS.

W. B. HATHAWAY, Proprietor.

Special Attention to the wants of Cyclists.

Special Rates to L. A. W. Men.

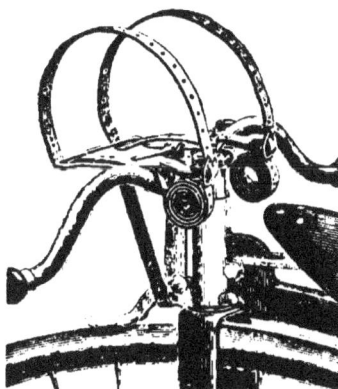

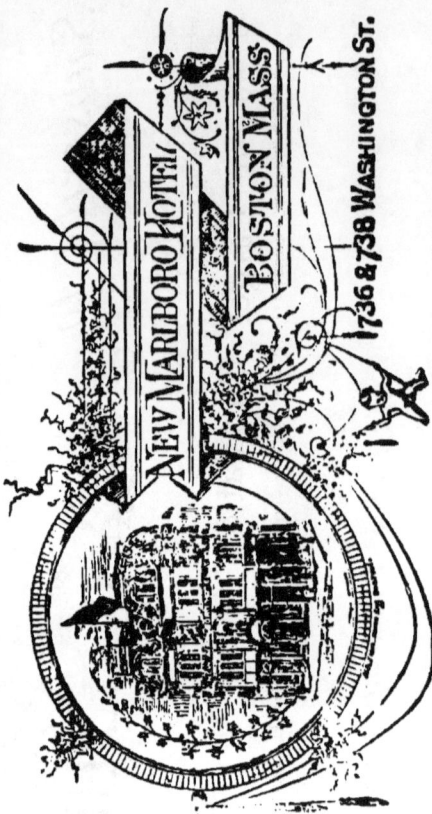

BAILEY'S HOTEL,

South Natick, Mass.,

Fifteen Miles from Boston.

GOOD ROADS THROUGH A DELIGHTFUL COUNTRY
ALL THE WAY.

$2.50 per day.

Dinner, 75 cents.

Lodging, 75 cents.

Special Attention to the Comfort and Accommodation of

WHEELMEN.

GOOD BOATING AND BATHING.

A. Bailey, Proprietor.

Bicycles Made to Order.

We are prepared to make Bicycles to order from your own designs. We have the largest stock of English parts to select from in the Trade. We have fitted our works with steam power, and with the aid of our Special Tools and Skilled Mechanics, we can finish all orders with promptness. We give a written guarantee with all our Machines.

In REPAIRING. NICKEL PLATING AND PAINTING

www.ingramcontent.com/pod-product-compliance
Lightning Source LLC
Chambersburg PA
CBHW021635270326
41931CB00008B/1043